Rookie Read-About® Science

It's a Good Thing There Are
Spiders

by Lisa M. Herrington

Content Consultant
Elizabeth Case DeSantis, M.A. Elementary Education
Julia A. Stark Elementary School, Stamford, Connecticut

Reading Consultant
Jeanne Clidas, Ph.D.
Reading Specialist

Children's Press®
An Imprint of Scholastic Inc.
New York Toronto London Auckland Sydney
Mexico City New Delhi Hong Kong
Danbury, Connecticut

Library of Congress Cataloging-in-Publication Data
Herrington, Lisa M., author.
It's a good thing there are spiders/by Lisa M. Herrington.
    pages cm. — (Rookie read-about science)
Summary: "Introduces the reader to spiders and explains the roles they play in the
environment."— Provided by publisher.
Audience: Ages 3-6.
ISBN 978-0-531-22360-4 (library binding: alk. paper) — ISBN 978-0-531-22832-6 (pbk.: alk. paper)
    1. Spiders —Juvenile literature. I. Title. II. Title: It is a good thing there are spiders. III. Series:
Rookie read-about science.

  QL458.4.H47 2015
  595.44—dc23   2014014971

Produced by Spooky Cheetah Press
Design by Keith Plechaty

© 2015 by Scholastic Inc.

Photographs ©: Alamy Images/stockex: 28 bottom; Dreamstime/Tomatito26: cover; Science
Source: 8, 31 center top (Dr. Keith Wheeler), 19 (Fabio Pupin/FLPA), 24 bottom right (Fletcher &
Baylis), 7 (Francesco Tomasinelli), 24 bottom left (Gregory G. Dimijian, M.D.), 16, 28 center (John
Serrao), 23 top (Mark Smith), 29 (Scott Linstead); Shutterstock, Inc.: 24 top right (FloridaStock),
3 top left (papkin), 28 top (Peter Waters); Superstock, Inc.: 31 center bottom (Animals Animals),
27 top left (Clarence Holmes/age fotostock), 20 (FLPA), 24 top left (imagebroker.net), 31 bottom
(Minden Pictures), 23 bottom (National Geographic), 27 bottom (NaturePL), 12 (NHPA), 11, 31 top
(Stock Connection), 15 (Tim Graham/Robert Harding Picture Library), 4 (Tips Images); Thinkstock:
30 top left (Anton Foltin), 3 top right (GlobalP), 27 top right (Jupiterimages), 3 bottom (Okea), 30
top right (shirophoto); Zara Environmental LLC/Dr. Jean K. Krejca: 30 bottom.

Table of Contents

It's a Good Thing...

Spiders may look scary. Many people are afraid of these creepy-crawlies. But it's a good thing there are spiders!

Tarantulas are the biggest spiders in the world.

Spiders eat insects that harm crops and plants. They are also food for birds, frogs, and other animals.

A wolf spider eats a grasshopper.

7.

Spiders make **silk**. It is very strong and stretchy. Scientists hope to copy how spiders make silk. Human-made silk may one day be used to help doctors fix wounds. It may also be used to make bulletproof vests for the military.

FUN FACT!

A spider can build a regular round web in about an hour.

What Are Spiders?

Many people think spiders are insects. But they are not. Spiders are **arachnids** (ah-RAK-nidz). Arachnids have eight legs. They also have two body parts—a head and an abdomen.

Scorpions and ticks are also arachnids.

head

legs

abdomen

egg sac

A mother spider lays eggs. She wraps them in silk to make an egg sac. Some spiders guard their egg sacs. Others carry the sacs around with them.

Baby spiders hatch from the eggs. They are called **spiderlings**.

Most spiders live about one year.
Tarantulas can live more than 20 years.

Spiders have small openings in the back of their bodies. They are called **spinnerets**. Liquid silk flows from them and dries into strong, thin threads. All spiders spin silk. Some use it to build webs.

Some spiders spin a line of silk to drop out of sight if they are in danger.

Feeding Time

Most spiders eat insects. They trap them in their sticky webs. Although most spiders have eight eyes, many cannot see well. Special hairs on their bodies and legs help them feel if an insect is caught in their web.

This spider wraps an insect in silk before eating it.

17

A spider uses its sharp fangs to bite and poison the insect. Spiders cannot chew as we do. So they drink juices from inside the insect.

Crab spiders can change their color to match a flower. This lets them sneak up on insects.

This tarantula chased down a tree frog.

Not all spiders weave webs to catch food. Some spiders—like tarantulas—hunt insects. They are even big enough to eat birds, mice, and frogs.

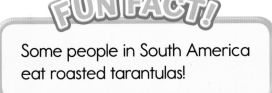

FUN FACT!

Some people in South America eat roasted tarantulas!

Many Kinds of Spiders

There are more than 30,000 kinds of spiders in the world. Spiders are everywhere. They live in forests, deserts, and caves. They are found in gardens and yards. Some may even live in your home.

The spider in the top photo lives in the desert. The one in the bottom is found in the rain forest.

Tarantula

Orb weaver

green lynx spider

banana spider

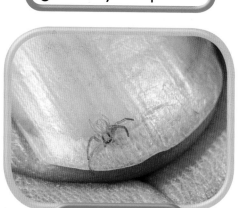

crab spider

giant crab spider

Spiders come in many shapes and sizes. They can be as tiny as a pinhead or as big as a dinner plate. Some are brown or black. Others are brightly colored.

FUN FACT!

Spiders can walk on walls and ceilings because they have special pads on their feet.

Big or small, spiders help us in many ways. It's a good thing there are spiders!

Spiders Are Good For...

...eating insects.

...providing food for animals like birds and frogs.

...offering clues about how to make strong silk.

The most venomous spider in the United States is the **black widow**. It has a red hourglass mark on its body. It is shy and attacks only if it is in danger.

Fishing spiders live near freshwater. Can you guess what they eat?

The **hairy wolf spider** gives her babies a piggyback ride.

Feature Fun

A **jumping spider** can leap huge distances for its food.

RIDDLES

Q. What computer job does a spider have?

A. Web designer!

Q. How is a spider like a toy top?

A. It is always spinning!

Creature Feature Fun

Which habitat is right for spiders?

A

B

Answer: A. Spiders could not survive out in the middle of the ocean.

Spiders Get a Hand

A rare type of eyeless spider was recently found in Texas. Scientists thought the spider had died out. At the time of the discovery, a road was being built in the area. The plans were changed. Now the road will not run through the spiders' home.

Glossary

arachnids (ah-RAK-nidz): animals with two body parts and eight legs

silk (silk): a strong thread that spiders make to build webs, homes, and egg sacs

spiderlings (SPY-dur-lings): baby spiders

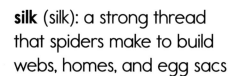

spinnerets (spin-ur-ETS): openings at the back of a spider's body where silk comes out

Index

Facts for Now

Visit this Scholastic Web site for more information on spiders:
www.factsfornow.scholastic.com
Enter the keyword **Spiders**

About the Author

Lisa M. Herrington writes books and articles for kids. She lives in Trumbull, Connecticut, with her husband, Ryan, and daughter, Caroline. She isn't scared of spiders. They fascinate her!